SCHOLASTIC

Let's Find Out™

Let's Explore the Five Senses

With City Dog and Country Dog

Laine Falk
Joan Michael

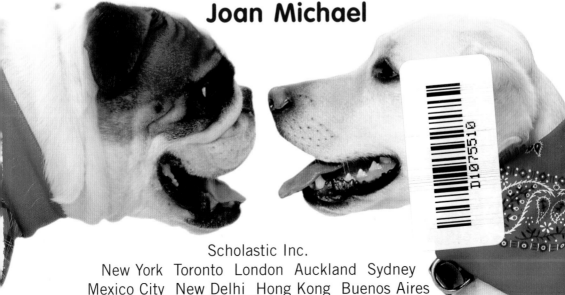

Scholastic Inc.
New York Toronto London Auckland Sydney
Mexico City New Delhi Hong Kong Buenos Aires

Literacy Specialist: Francie Alexander, Chief Academic Officer, Scholastic Inc.

Art Director: Joan Michael

Photographs: all dog photos by James Levin
©Joe Kingleigh/Getty Images (p3 city image); ©Panoramic Images/Getty Images (p3 cows grazing); ©Oote Boe/Alamy (pp4-5 pedestrians); ©Dynamic Graphics/Creatas/Alamy (pp6-7 girl with goat); ©Steve Hamblin/Alamy (pp8-9 Times Square); ©David Ponton/Getty Images (p10-11 path in forest); ©Ambient Images Inc/Alamy (pp12-13 Union Square Market); ©Richard Price/Getty Images (pp14-15 barndyard); ©Photodic via SODA (p15 cow); ©Pixonnet.com/Alamy (pp16-17 hot dog cart); ©Photodisc (p16 hot dog in Charlie's mouth); ©Andrew Hetherington/Getty Images; (pp18-19 field); ©Jules Frazier/Getty Images (p18 water bucket); ©Taylor S. Kennedy/Getty Images (pp20-21 train on stone bridge); ©altrendo nature/Getty Images (pp22-23 outdoor scene); ©Photodisc (p23 soccer ball)

Copyright © 2006 by Scholastic Inc.
All rights reserved.   Printed in China.
Published by Scholastic Inc.

LET'S FIND OUT, LET'S FIND OUT EARLY LEARNING BOOKS, and SCHOLASTIC and associated logos are trademarks and/or registered trademarks of Scholastic Inc.

ISBN 0-439-91581-3

1 2 3 4 5 6 7 8 9 10   62   14 13 12 11 10 09 08 07 06

Charlie

is a city dog.
What does he
see, hear, smell,
taste, and feel
in the city?

Buttercup

is a country dog.
What does she see,
hear, smell, taste, and
feel in the country?

City Dog

Charlie sees
with his eyes.

Charlie sees crowds of
people in the city.

coming through!

In the country, Buttercup sees something shiny. What does Buttercup see?

Beautiful!

Country Dog
Buttercup
sees with her eyes.

Buttercup sees shiny ribbons
at the fair in the country.

In the city, Charlie hears something loud.
What does Charlie hear?

City Dog

Charlie hears
with his ears.

Charlie hears horns honking
in the city.

In the country, Buttercup hears something singing. What does Buttercup hear?

In the city, Charlie smells something sweet.
What does Charlie smell?

Sniff!

City Dog

Charlie smells
with his nose.

Charlie smells flowers at the
outdoor market in the city.

In the country, Buttercup smells something fresh. What does Buttercup smell?

Buttercup smells fresh-cut hay in the country.

In the city, Charlie tastes something yummy. What does Charlie taste?

Chomp!
Chomp!

City Dog

Charlie tastes with his tongue.

Charlie tastes a juicy hot dog in the city.

In the country, Buttercup tastes something wet and cold. What does Buttercup taste?

Slurp!

Country Dog
Buttercup tastes with her tongue.

Buttercup tastes water from a pump in the country.

Slurp!

In the city, Charlie feels something cool.
What does Charlie feel?

BUT WAIT!
Charlie's not in the city!
He's taking a trip
on a train.

City Dog

Charlie feels
with his skin.

He feels the wind on his face
as he rides the train.

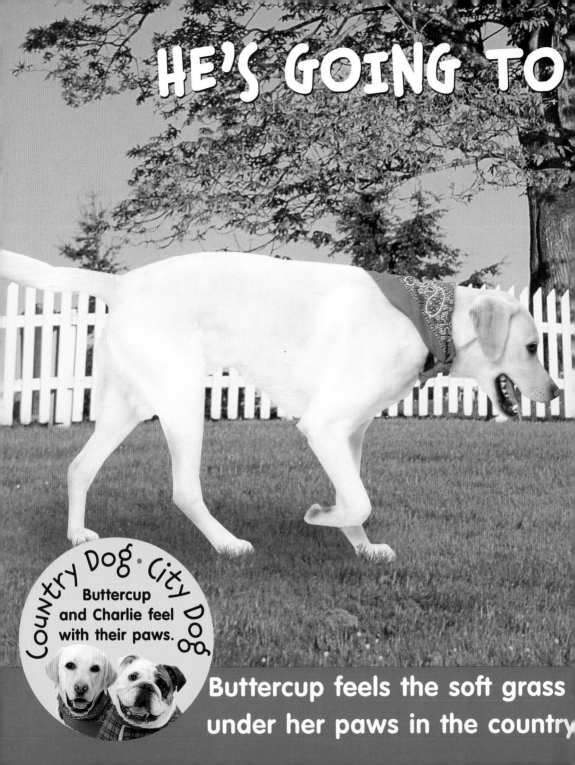

HE'S GOING TO

Country Dog · City Dog

Buttercup and Charlie feel with their paws.

Buttercup feels the soft grass under her paws in the country

SEE BUTTERCUP!

Charlie feels the soft grass under his paws too.

Charlie and Buttercup use their five senses.

They see with their eyes.

They hear with their ears.

They smell with their noses.

They taste with their tongues.

They feel with their skin and paws.

How do you see, hear, smell, taste, and feel?
How did you use your five senses today?